To:

_____

From Your Friend:

_____

No Better *Friend* Than *You*

paintings by

D. Morgan®

H

HARVEST HOUSE PUBLISHERS

EUGENE, OREGON

No Better *Friend* Than *You*

Text Copyright © 2004 by Harvest House Publishers
Eugene, Oregon 97402

ISBN 0-7369-1266-5

Artwork © D. Morgan by arrangement with Grace Licensing in Bainbridge, Indiana. For more information regarding art prints featured in this book, please contact Grace Licensing at 1-877-210-3456.

Design and production by Koechel Peterson & Associates, Inc., Minneapolis, Minnesota

Scripture quotations are taken from the Holy Bible, New International Version®, Copyright © 1973, 1978, 1984 by the International Bible Society. Used by permission of Zondervan Publishing House. All rights reserved.

Harvest House Publishers has made every effort to trace the ownership of all poems and quotes. In the event of a question arising from the use of a poem or quote, we regret any error made and will be pleased to make the necessary correction in future editions of this book.

Printed in China

04 05 06 07 08 09 10 11 12 / IM / 10 9 8 7 6 5 4 3 2 1

DEDICATION

Peggy, this book is dedicated to you,
my dearest friend in all the world.
As soul mates since we were six years old,
we've seen the owl and heard the wolf.
Our steadfast friendship is forever.
Our "ventures" will never end,
they are truly just around the bend.

Love forever. . .your huckleberry friend,
Doris

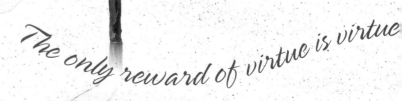

*L*ove is all very well
in its way, but
friendship is
much higher.
Indeed, I know of
nothing in the world
that is either nobler
or rarer than a
devoted friendship.

OSCAR WILDE

The only reward of virtue is virtue

the only way to have a friend is to be one.

RALPH WALDO EMERSON

D. Morgan © 2002

Friendship is the source of the greatest pleasures, and without friends even the most agreeable pursuits become tedious.

THOMAS AQUINAS

D. Morgan®

The greatest sweetener of human life is Friendship. To raise this to the highest pitch of enjoyment, is a secret which but few discover.

JOSEPH ADDISON

Friends are an aid to the young,
    To guard them from error;
To the elderly,
    To attend to their wants and to supplement
        their failing power of action;
To those in the prime of life,
    To assist them in noble deeds.

ARISTOTLE

Go in peace, for we have sworn friendship with each other in the name of the Lord.

THE BOOK OF 1 SAMUEL

Friendship is a serious affection;
the most sublime of all affections,
because it is founded on principle,
and cemented by time.

MARY WOLLSTONECRAFT

Friendship takes place between those who have an affinity for one another, and is a perfectly natural and inevitable result

HENRY DAVID THOREAU

One who forgives an affront fosters friendship, but one who dwells on disputes will alienate a friend.

THE BOOK OF PROVERBS

The Impossible Dream......Isn't.

D. Morgan ©1996

*B*e courteous to all, but intimate with few, and let those few be well tried before you give them your confidence. True friendship is a plant of slow growth, and must undergo and withstand the shocks of adversity before it is entitled to the appellation.

GEORGE WASHINGTON

The uglier we get in the eyes of others, the lovelier we shall be to each other that has always been my firm faith about friendship.

GEORGE ELIOT

Trust in my affection for you.

ANNEA JAMESON

Friends we were — Friends we are —

Friends we'll always be.

D. Morgan © 1996

A friendship that like love is warm;
A love like friendship, steady.

THOMAS MOORE

Hearts are linked to hearts by God. The friend on whose fidelity you can count, whose success in life flushes your cheek with honest satisfaction, whose triumphant career you have traced and read with a heart throbbing almost as if it were a thing alive, for whose honor you would answer as for your own— that friend, given to you by circumstances over which you have no control, was God's own gift.

FREDERIC WILLIAM ROBERTSON

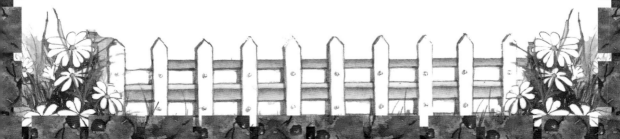

Friendship is the greatest of worldly goods.
Certainly to me it is the chief happiness of life.

C.S. LEWIS

Friendship is
certainly the
finest balm for
the pangs of
disappointed love.

JANE AUSTEN

Welcome friend... Settle in .....
Shed a tear ... Share a grin
With each new morning
Come what may ~

God is just A Prayer Away.

D. Morgan®

Friendship is the union of spirits, a marriage

D. Morgan ©1990

When true friends meet in adverse hour;
'Tis like a sunbeam through a shower.
A watery way an instant seen,
The darkly closing clouds between.

SIR WALTER SCOTT

of hearts, and the bond thereof virtue. WILLIAM PENN

Your friends will know you better in the first minute you meet than your acquaintances will know you in a thousand years.

RICHARD BACH

*F*riendship! mysterious cement of the soul!
Sweetener of life! and solder of society!

ROBERT BLAIR

Through the seasons, through the years,
it's your friends who carry you through.

EMILIE BARNES

Colder

As the world grows

Here's my shoulder

...Lean On Me.

D. Morgan ©2002

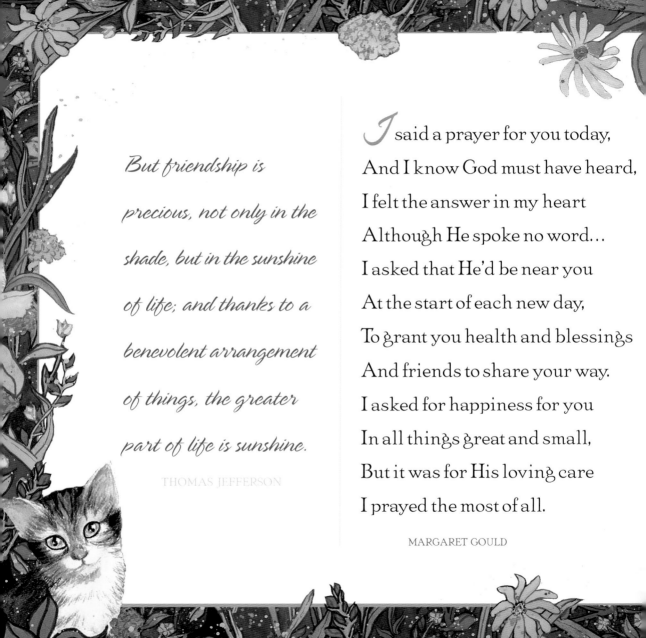

But friendship is precious, not only in the shade, but in the sunshine of life; and thanks to a benevolent arrangement of things, the greater part of life is sunshine.

THOMAS JEFFERSON

I said a prayer for you today,
And I know God must have heard,
I felt the answer in my heart
Although He spoke no word…
I asked that He'd be near you
At the start of each new day,
To grant you health and blessings
And friends to share your way.
I asked for happiness for you
In all things great and small,
But it was for His loving care
I prayed the most of all.

MARGARET GOULD

From quiet homes and first beginning,
out to the undiscovered ends,
there's nothing worth the wear of winning,
but laughter and the love of friends.

HILAIRE BELLOC

*F*riendship is a compact in which one fairly shares defects and merits. We may judge of friends, whether man or woman, giving them credit for what is good, and overlooking what is bad in them, appreciating them at their just value, while giving ourselves up to an intimate, intense and charming sympathy.

GUY DE MAUPASSANT

Love ......will light ...... your way.

D. Morgan © 1989

*B*e a friend. You don't need money;
Just a disposition sunny;
Just the wish to help another
Get along some way or other;
Just a kindly hand extended
Out to one who's unbefriended;
Just the will to give or lend,
This will make you someone's friend.

*B*e a friend. You don't need glory.
Friendship is a simple story.
Pass by trifling errors blindly,
Gaze on honest effort kindly,
Cheer the youth who's bravely trying,
Pity him who's sadly sighing;
Just a little labor spend
On the duties of a friend.

*B*e a friend. The pay is bigger
(Though not written by a figure)
Than is earned by people clever
In what's merely self-endeavor.
You'll have friends instead of neighbors
For the profits of your labors;
You'll be richer in the end
Than a prince, if you're a friend.

EDGAR GUEST

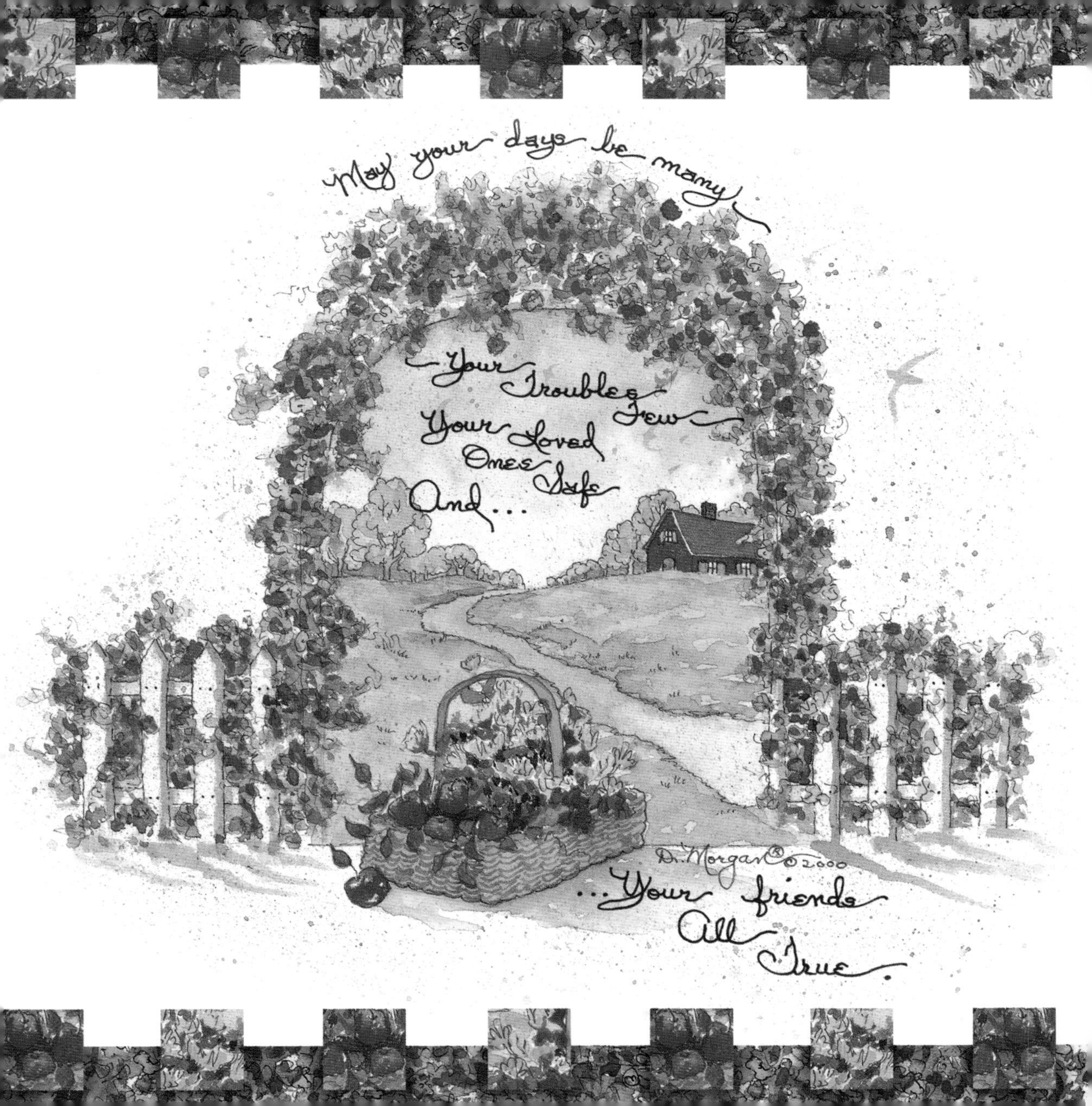

May your days be many

Your Troubles Few
Your Loved
Ones Safe
And...

...Your friends
All
True

D. Morgan © 2000

It is not until you have the courage to engage
in human relationships that you grow.

GARY ZUKAV

Friendship throws out deep roots in honest hearts

ALEXANDER DUMAS

Treasure each other
in the recognition
that we do not know
how long we shall
have each other.

JOSHUA LOTH LIEBMAN

In my friend, I find a second self.

ISABEL NORTON

The rule of friendship means there should be mutual sympathy between them, each supplying what the other lacks and trying to benefit the other, always using friendly and sincere words.

MARCUS TULLIUS CICERO

My best friend is the one who brings out the best in me.

HENRY FORD

Friends minister to each other, nurse each other. Friends give to each other, worry about each other, stand always ready to help. Perfect friendship is rarely achieved, but at its height it is an ecstasy.

STEPHEN E. AMBROSE

There you are.

In the best of my dreams...

D. Morgan ©1992

The Friendship Chain

A friendship chain has many links
 Connected one by one,
And through the length, and breadth of it
 Electric currents run.
Some links are made of solid gold
 Of real intrinsic worth,
And these are treasured as the best
 Of any on the earth.

And some are made of silver bright
 Of sterling merit pure,
And valued well, because they will
 Throughout all time endure.
Still others seeming naught but lead
 Of dull and homely hue,
Have iron hearts, that ever prove
 To be both good and true.

And many are the links on links
 Of some material plain,
That worthy are to hold a place
 In this true friendship chain.
For when life's waves by troubles tossed
 Dash wild upon the shore,
They hold the frail bark anchored well
 Until the storm is o'er.

Come wind or calm, come joy or woe,
 Come dull or pleasant weather,
The links retain the same strong hold
 That keeps the chain together.
For if perchance, through lapse of years
 Some links may broken be,
The chain will never break, because
 They hold invisibly.

JOSEPHINE CURRIER

May all your dreams come true.

D. Morgan ©1992

You'll always be my special friend.

D. Morgan © 1994